SO QUIETLY
THE EARTH

BOOKS BY DAVID LEE

So Quietly the Earth (Copper Canyon Press, 2004)

Incident at Thompson Slough (Wood Works Press, 2002)

News from Down to the Cafe: New Poems (Copper Canyon Press, 1999)

A Legacy of Shadows: Selected Poems (Copper Canyon Press, 1999)

David Lee: A Listener's Guide (Copper Canyon Press, 1999)

Twenty-one Gun Salute (Grey Spider Press, 1999)

The Fish (Wood Works Press, 1997)

Wayburne Pig (Brooding Heron Press, 1997)

Covenants (with William Kloefkorn) (Spoon River Poetry Press, 1996)

My Town (Copper Canyon Press, 1995)

Paragonah Canyon (Brooding Heron Press, 1990)

Day's Work (Copper Canyon Press, 1990)

The Porcine Canticles (Copper Canyon Press, 1984)

Shadow Weaver (Brooding Heron Press, 1984)

Driving and Drinking (Copper Canyon Press, 1979)

Porcine Legacy (Copper Canyon Press, 1974)

SO QUIETLY
THE EARTH

DAVID LEE

COPPER CANYON PRESS

Cover art: *Devil's Garden,* photograph by Jack Hollingsworth/Getty Images.

Copper Canyon Press is in residence under the auspices of the Centrum Foundation at Fort Worden State Park in Port Townsend, Washington. Centrum sponsors artist residencies, education workshops for Washington State students and teachers, Blues, Jazz, and Fiddle Tunes festivals, classical music performances, and the Port Townsend Writers' Conference.

Library of Congress Cataloging-in-Publication Data

Lee, David, 1944 Aug. 13–
  So quietly the earth / David Lee.
    p. cm.
ISBN 1-55659-204-3 (alk. paper)
1. Southwestern States—Poetry 2. Human ecology—Poetry.
3. Landscape—Poetry. 4. Nature—Poetry. I. Title.
PS3562.E338S6 2004
811'.54—dc22

                     2003024719

98765432
FIRST PRINTING

COPPER CANYON PRESS
Post Office Box 271
Port Townsend, Washington 98368
www.coppercanyonpress.org

ACKNOWLEDGMENTS

My thanks to the editors of the following magazines and presses in which poems from this book have previously appeared: *Alaska Quarterly Review, Brooding Heron Press, Crab Creek Review, Kayak, Land That We Love, Midwest Quarterly, 911, Petroglyph, Sabella, Salt Lake Magazine, Silver Vain Magazine, The Soul Unearthed, The Spoon River Poetry Press, Tailwind, Voicings from the High Country, Weber Studies,* and *Willow Springs Magazine.*

Special thanks to Rob Behuin, Doug Bonzo, Joan Coles, Michael Donovan, Sam Green, Paul Hunter, William Kloefkorn, JoDee Lee, Jon Lee, and Eleanor Wilner for technical advice, critique, and encouragement along the way. *Gracias, amigos.* And to Michael Wiegers for splendid editorial advice and consultation. *Estupendo.* And to Jan, fellow road warrior, *te quiero.*

Some of these poems found their genesis while the poet was attending a National Endowment for the Humanities Institute for Studies in the Southwest at Southwest Texas State University; thanks to Mark Busby and the NEH. The book's structure came to light while the poet was preparing for and attending a symposium, "Religion, Science, and Literature and their relationship to Planet Earth," at the American Academy of Arts and Sciences; thanks to Gary Holthaus and Harvard University.

for

Pauline Bulloch

Leslie and Kitty Norris

Ken and Jane Sleight

with love

CONTENTS

2

The hidden God is far above every outward thing and every thought, and is found only where thou hidest thyself in the secret place of the heart, in the quiet solitude where no word is spoken, where is neither creature nor image nor fancy. This is the quiet Desert of the Godhead, the Divine Darkness.

R.M. Jones, *Studies in Mystical Religion*

To see a World in a Grain of Sand
And a Heaven in a Wild Flower

William Blake

Solvitur ambulando
(*It can be solved while walking*)

Saint Augustine

Canyonlands Requiem

In the rust-colored edge of my life
I come here to find myself.
I am your child, the living myth
of this dream we call reality,
a part of the story, a foreshadowing
of its conclusion.
Having only this remaining
as my strength
now I lay me down these words
washed in the dreamshadows
of hope, contradiction, and goodbye.

I

*I praise the earth, the wide-stretched, the traversable,
the vast, the unbounded, thy mother, O righteous
Homa!*

Homa Yast

We did not regard the mountains and forests as wilderness; we called it home.

Luther Standing Bear

*Earth: Mother of the Gods,
the wife of the starry Heaven.*

Homer, Hymn 30

*By earth is meant the Lord's church in the heavens and
on the earth: the church, wherever it may be, is the
Lord's kingdom.*

Emanuel Swedenborg

Dawn Psalm, Pine Valley

1

While I was not watching
sunrise came with a ruby throat
and gold-flecked wings.

2

Blue
and a small wisp of cloud
above the dark pine.
A jaysquall
leaves a small bruise
on one corner
of sky.

3

Boiling coffee.
A blue enamel pot
nestled in warm coals
beside the cold
sliding water.
Sky so close
you fear
bumping your head.

4

A brown breaks surface
rising to wingshadow
drifting on the blue selvage
of pond.

5

Golden lace.
Sunrise pours slantwise
into clear water
through the blue spruce,
the deep tangle of pine
and purled woodsmoke.

6

I turned
and the earth hushed.
While I leaned into silence
a morning too vast to fathom
filled with light.

7

Praise.

Alpine Pond, Cedar Breaks

Joy, fair spark of the gods
Daughter of Elysium!
Drunk with fiery rapture, Goddess,
We approach thy shrine!

Friedrich Schiller

Just before dawn the sky darkens. Barely
perceptible. At times on the ocean or great plains
a green flash follows. Prelude. Or anthem.
And then sun. Up again, spilling through
this maze of pine and aspen
into the free sculpture of fluted ridges, hoodoos,
and weathered earth. Below me a breastbone
for the winds, cirque rising out of cirque
until the small pond beneath the rim
loosely holding the essence of blue. Shadows
seep a red darkness as colors awaken.

The pond is still, only the sound of water.
All around a trickle. A gurgle from the snowfield
on a frail summer grass. A splash
from the creek etched on the west wall, which
moves down toward broken sandstone.
Pinnacles, spires, and glowing rock.
The convergence of two worlds
demands trumpets, strings, timpani, a
flood of grandeur. *Allegro ma non troppo; Presto.*
And the soaring of human voice, the fountainhead.
Deliverance through joy. Music pours
over the Breaks, symphony and chorale:
                    Freude, schöner Götterfunken.
Dawn spreads the high country. Day breaks.

Behind, a shrill whistle. A fat marmot
stands on his boulder, watching, tiny paws
clasped before his chest, dark eyes glistening.

A gray camp robber clatters from its spruce perch.
The venerable hotai stiffens, lifts his chin,
whistles again. I whistle back. Almost, I see
him smile *aha! You silly!* almost, bow. I nod
for the both of us. Once more for the bird.
The marmot turns away, disappears
in broken ground. No sound from the trees.
A slow *shissh* as dawnwind clambers over
the Breaks. I go on, sitting still as the old
sun makes its way. For the moment
no inclination toward moving anywhere.

The Grand Staircase

Each person
Has one big theory to explain the universe
But it doesn't tell the whole story
And in the end it is what is outside him
That matters, to him and especially to us
Who have been given no help whatever
In decoding our own man-size quotient and must rely
On second-hand knowledge.

John Ashbery

A vast and primeval inland sea.
Sand and debris washed from the highlands,
sediment on the slippery film
of ocean floor. Water
forcing its weight downward, lime
and silica cementing these particles
into a mass of living rock.
The earth trembled,

convulsed great stone to the edge
of sea. Rivers
dragged their waters over
dihedrals. Marshes and lakes.
Ancient tides. A winter eon
and silence of brackish water.
Summer and swampy pastures,
lumbering dinosaurs. Layer
piled on layer as rivers and tides
built deeper, dark veins
of shale and sandstone rising
from a limestone pedestal.

Water broke on bedrock.
New seas splashed the earth.
A thousand feet of blood rock
over the chocolate belts.
Winds turned,
prehensile, tore down

a western mountain, drowned
the fertile sea in an inundation
of sand. Dunes choked rivers,
shallow lakes. The great desert
piled two thousand feet,
a riser of stone.

And the sea returned.

A shallow re-invasion teemed
with shellfish, reptiles.
Bodies mixed with sand, leached
iron pigment from desert rock,
metamorphosed to a plane
of carmel lime, solidified.
The land yawned,
toyed with sea.
Sandbanks and gravel covered
mud and silt. A drab winter
crossed horizon.
Under a long cloudless night
earth slumbered in gray dreams
until birds called the sky
and the land stirred. Sea
drained away. Mountains folded
with the waking, thrust heavenward.
Clear water in bowls of stone between.
Rivers drained from highlands

eroding fragile ribs, carrying
the mountains grain by grain
to inland lakes. A pink sediment
spread the earth.

The land rose. In a great arch
it swelled two miles above the belly
of sea. Rivers carried away rock strata,
dug into earth. And the land
broke, dividing into great pieces,

plateaus, etched by deep fault lines
where rock separated,
valleys and basins. Delineaments.
Rains fell. Seasons turned. Winds
came. The earth breathed.

Paragonah in the Rhythm of Birdsong

Meadowlark call trilling softly,
a moving sky at my doorway.
Jan's mountain ash huddles by the back porch.
Its fallen leaves in the yellow grass
cling to the quiet earth.

Idyll: Found Poem

on coming upon a child
   squatting by a hawk moth
      drawn by the nectar of an Oenothera
         on the path to Calf Creek Falls

What
I meant to say
have you found?

Look
he shouted clearly
what I discovered!

While Walking (1)

3 John 4

The wind is happy today.
How do you know?
Listen. She's singing.

Summer Count: *Wyethia arizonica*

after Bashō

Yellow Indian tobacco: mules-ears
all across Whipple Meadow.
No elk today.

Abandoned Cabin on the Clark Ranch: Solstice

Here's a marvail's convenient
place for our rehearsal.

A Midsummer Night's Dream, 3.1.2–3

1

Dark slides back, pools under the iron bed frame,
the crumbling stove, lurks in exposed joists.
A nail of sharp light through a missing shingle
cockeyed in the afternoon sun
angles the room as it huddles beneath
a caving truss, ceiling and floor in abeyance.
From the small east window, darkness empties
into clear day and the distance of green canyon,
then Cedar Breaks, the pink and orange badlands.
In the center a gray table, groaning chairs:
the eye slowly fills the four corners of room.

2

So then: Peter Quince: architect, carpenter, divine.
And on this June day a lost piece of sun
transfixes this chamber; tonight a point
of moonlight sweeps the wood floor. But the dust
is not stirred. Within the carpentry
of this one-room mountain cabin
in this dream of a man at a table
in a yellow-walled study in his house
sharing memory with wind, dust lies still
in the moonlit apartment of the forehead.

3

In the stage set of the mind
a gray table centered on the floor
delineates the chambers of Peter's cabin: kitchen,
bedroom, den, hallway, sharp north, falling south.

Beyond the cleavage of warping pine
the window frames canyon, gnarled Breaks,
a rising almost transparent moon,
and brilliant wall of blue sky, the rock
upon which this dream is built.

On Turning Up a Fossil in My Garden

Natural extinction need not connote
a forced or meaningless fall into oblivion:
instead, one of the simple facts of life, the ultimate
fate of all species, not tainted by a stigma
of failure: like breath, frequent in occurrence
but unworthy of inordinate praise, not
especially provocative as conversation. As
when two lovers cease their heavy breathing, and part,
and the moonlight seeps into a darkened room:
seen clearly with no apprehension, animosity, fear.

Cedar Breaks

It began as silt deposits in shallow freshwater lakes. The earth shuddered,
began a slow climb, a swelling. A piece uplifted, slid apart from the old
lakebed, rose. Then a great sea covered the land. A million years later,
naked strata loom on the eastern horizon as if waiting the perpetual thrust
of a copper moon, tilting the autumn sky. Geologic debris. At Sunset
Point, 10,000 feet above sea level, it is a short walk through a petrified
oyster bed to bristlecone pine, perhaps the world's oldest living things.
Farther down the lip, a cluster of gnarled ancients, one a warped
bifurcation. In the cleavage a hummingbird's nest, two tiny eggs. Far
below in a gray tangle of city, a young woman closes her eyes to the warm
half-light, her breast exposed, kissed.

While Walking (11)

Revelation 12:1–2

Are all songs happy?
No. Sometimes when the moon sings it's because she's sad.

Postcard to Sam from Paragonah

The red hills open to let in the wind.
Dust floats through the oak underbrush
then sweeps away in alternate currents
to the sky's corner where a hawk screes
then folds and comes down blind, moves
from one myopic association to another
rising and shrieking, now quickly gone
and swallowed by the cracks and stains
of high rock. The wind writhes again,
moves down the canyon, an insane woman
clawing against the skin of her lover.
You can sit for hours, friend, letting
it all enter. The rip current carries
your voice as far as you want. You can
touch the mixing clouds, taste the raw
earth. When you come down the red dirt
rests easy in the lines of your hands.

Aspen Pole Fence

The aspen poles crisscross, a zigzag line
slicing the dry belly of the meadow, five high
at one hundred twenty degree angles compounded.
Such waste in a pragmatic sense. Consider
materials: five aspen poles per section at, say,
twenty feet per pole. With angles, six sections builds
approximately eighty feet of fence, a net loss of two
sections, ten aspen poles. But the gained strength.
And durability. Chester said the old Horse Valley
fence stood seventy years, which means fifty, until
Forest Service knocked the east side down, let
Job Corps put up sheep mesh, which went over
in the second year's snow. And the aesthetics.
Gods. The beauty of a cross-pole fence in autumn.

But the trees. The beautiful aspen cut wholesale
for such a piece of geometry: five poles per section
when one pole equals one tree once living now
one pole. Chester said there are plenty of aspen
in the first place and in the second some things
have to be sacrificed in the name of progress
and in the third that land belongs to him. Which
means the trees. Unless they can find a way to leave.
Which is why he built that fence in the first place:
so things wouldn't be getting away. They're only
trash trees. You can't get rid of them when you try.

Why is it that for some things there is partial sacrifice,
while others are required to give up all? At night I can believe
shadows of aspen trees grope along the far side
of the fence. I have not gone to see. In autumn,
when aspen spread the earth gold, I can think
the gray skeleton sprawling across yellow grass
is a good thing, Chester's fat sheep mindlessly
following its confines from one corner to the next,
to water, and back out toward the fence.
A completion, a perfect holding pattern. Then

always I see its direction: the aspen grove flowing
down the west hill, a twisted gray arm stretching
out toward the glistening splash of autumn color.

Idyll for a Collapsing Season

The barn
fallen to its knees.

From a failed splice
in the torn east wall
a spew of

musty hay and molded grain
rancid oats and a skein
of ruined rope

a broken-handled pitchfork
and an ossified length of tack
twisted like a devil's sputum

seasoned with half a century's
rat turds

a rusted plowshare
and a lynched god's ransom
of ancient baling wire
moaning in the dry wind

detritus cast forth across
the abandoned corral

a banshee's cornucopia
under the huddled
November sky.

While Walking (III)

1 Corinthians 14:7

How do you know she's sad?
Haven't you heard her? Listen.

Autumn

A red-tailed hawk
hangs on a tattered gray cloud
delineating the wind,
a bright leaf caught
in the bellyfur of a torn storm.

Yovimpa Point

for my father

Job 17:13

A stiff, pine-scented wind. The tough
gnarled trees behind me creak and groan.
Swallows dart from the pink cliffs,
swoop over the escarpment and wheel
through the maze of orange hoodoos.
Three thousand square miles of high desert
fall into southern horizon, down the staircase
to the Coconino where the Kaibab Plateau
hides the great chasm. On the eastern
circumference, the dome of Navajo Mountain
under a hazy sky. Westward,
Mount Trumbull huddles low against the earth.

Through this space I stare into the eye
of time. The rocks I stand upon are young,
rugged, weathered only twenty million years.
A thousand feet beneath this crenation
bland gray cliffs mark one hundred fifty million years
and on the near horizon the deep hue
of vermilion rose upon the belted strata
two hundred million years past. All rest
on a base of limestone twenty-five million years
preceding even that.

          A vast ocean. A marsh
where giant ferns nodded in the sun and
great reptiles slithered into extinction.
A sleeping desert. A young mountain, thrusting
against a moving sky. The earth opens
before me.

Today once again, an ancient voice
in the wind calls, the same question

repeated: *Where wast thou when I laid*
the foundations of the earth? Declare,
if thou hast understanding.
Even in my silence, as I hold my arms
close against my sides, shivering
before the probing gust,
I grow more and more sure of my answer.
Here, Lord. I am here. In the beginning,
even now, here. Hues of pink and gold
beneath massive white formations fall
to green basin and the brilliant red horizon.
Gods. A world of gods, at play before me.

Bright Angel Point at Sunset

Thus the light rains, thus pours...
The liquid and rushing crystal
  beneath the knees of the gods.

Ezra Pound, Canto IV

The canyon bleeds, then deepens
and darkens. The intricate declension
of its ledges, bluffs, and grottoes
blends in this late light.
Wind swirls from the depths
carrying pine scent on its back.
A sliver of white moon
in the east. A nighthawk soars above.
Thin light spills into the gorge
and the river sings an ancient song.
At the edge of shadow, night:
dark stone, pine scent, water, cascading light.

Parowan Canyon

When granite and sandstone begin to blur
and flow, the eye rests on cool white aspen.
Strange, their seeming transparency.
How as in a sudden flash one remembers
a forgotten name, so the recollection. *Aspen.*
With a breeze in them, their quiet rhythms,
shimmering, quaking. Powder on the palm.
Cool on the cheek. Such delicacy
the brittle wood, limbs snapping
at a grasp, whole trees tumbling in the winds.
Sweet scent on a swollen afternoon.
Autumn, leaves falling one upon another, gold
rains upon a golden earth. How at evening
when the forest darkens, aspen do not.
And a white moon rises and silver stars
point toward the mountain, darkness
holds them so pale.
They stand still, very still.

While Walking (IV)

Isaiah 10:19

Do you think a tree cries when somebody cuts it down?
I don't know. Do you?
Yes.

Pit Stop at Parowan Gap on a Windy Night

The landscape here chaos, barren foothills
with gigantic upthrusts and clastic dikes,
as if some strange god plowed the earth
to mark an edge of wasteland. Beyond the gap
the sprawl of desert, its movement
imperceptible even in fat moonlight,
as if this god planned a sanctuary of broken stone
to its god, proportionate to its chosen place,
abandoned ramparts scattered in profusion.

Grand visions splay the sandstone walls.
Shades of men and beasts haunt the ancient
cathedral, etched into soft bowls of stone,
red and gray ledges. Miniature forms
leap in silhouette under a carved dangling sky,
creeping moon. Rains fall, seasons turn,
harsh winds bite into the crumbling rock.
An anthropomorph dances across the frozen back
of a rattler. Three strange creatures,
deerlike with flowing antlers
and sweeping tails, float beneath
a glowing sun, tall pine, the makers
gone, vanished into the expanse of distance.

From the road transversing the gap, ruin
is evident and everywhere, one eon's monument
another's graffito wall or pissing alley,
suppositions a plague of nightwind in the dissolving
geometry called *universe,* known by its bones
and our guesses. One blends into another,
stone upon stone, petroglyph overlaid on petroglyph,
as when a child erases with a Jumbo school pencil,
forever CAT rests on a COT until the Big Chief
wood-pulp tablet rots, crumbles in the drawer
to become no more than wind fodder,
then is mourned only for its absence, so
the lowered car lights shine into darkness,
the gravel road stretches toward oblivion.

Zion Narrows

Great stone walls shut out stars
to the east and west, loom and close
as night deepens. A breeze
stirs the willows. River.
Dark sandstone seems to breathe.
A thin new moon struggles
over the brooding cliffs
and glitters, askew
in the brimming water. Shadows lurk
in the cottonwoods. A night creature
slides into the clearing,
moves toward the river, seems to bend,
drink. It blends into sighing night,
the haunted canyon,
its warm wind,
crescent moon, shadows,
deep-throated song of water.

After the Tree Came Down

Was it
The world tree he was felling?
Was this the day?

Denise Levertov

Past the edge of evening,
between the rise of quarter moon
and midnight,
beyond the last echo
of trimming axe and chain saw,

I felt an injured woodspirit
outside my window
looking up into starlight,
her fingers reaching
into the dream of elmshadow,
as if grasping
for an ancient harp
hung in the branches
of sorrowing darkness.

She ran before I could turn
and when I called
into the bruised nightscape
I knew:
she will not look back.

Kaiparowits Plateau

Deep in their roots all flowers keep the light
Theodore Roethke

Tonight an enormous corn moon, fecund
and glistening, slides through a slow sky
over Navajo Mountain. Such undulations
this light, gliding the flat crest
of Fifty Mile, pulsing at the knees of Smoky Mountain,
almost a shimmering tide on the basin floor.

How long since
it seeped through the Cretaceous forest
into the nodding miles of blossoms
flowing across a tropical plain?

Tonight the mesa slumbers.
It dreams moonlight, metamorphosed,
hidden in the secret declivities, dark and moist
hollows. Its ancient forest broods in black silence.
Between gray rocks, from a small crack
in the sandstone plateau, a milkweed thrusts out
its yellow shoot, tastes the nightwind.

Psalm Written after Reading Cormac McCarthy and Taking a Three-Hour Climb to the Top of Pine Valley Mountain

Laughter is also a form of prayer
Søren Kierkegaard

Right here, Lord,
tether me to my shadow
like a fat, spavined mule
stuck sideways in tankmud
bawling for eternity.

At midnight,
when the stars slip their traces
and race the moon like wild horses
to their deaths in the darkness,
let my hoarse song twine with the nightwind.

May the bray
of today's laughter fall
like a pitchy topbranch from a tall yellow pine
straight down like winter sleet
to the mountain's bent and trembling knees.

2

For it is by earth that we see earth, and by water water, and by air glorious air; so too, by fire we see destroying fire.

  Empedocles

Who among us shall dwell with the devouring fire?
Who among us shall dwell with everlasting burnings?
He that walketh righteously, and speaketh uprightly...

  Isaiah 33:14–15

Then like the young sun on the eastern mountain or the fire when fanned by the wind, the prince gradually grew in all due perfection, like the moon in the fortnight of brightness.

  Buddha-charita 2.20

Dry Lightning: Thor, in Disguise, Searches for Freya

A tattered shadow
like the ghost of a lost child
peering into the desert
in search of the wandering moon
clings to the edge of horizon

then rises, full grown and angry,
to stride across the afternoon sky,
thickening the air.

Suddenly, as if a madman
escaped from the underworld
swung a six-thousand-pound sledge
into an eighty-ton block of obsidian
hung from a giant's noose
togglebolted to the sky,

the canyonlands ring
as the peal echoes through the stretch marks
of the earth's belly.

Sonnet on the Sun, Rising

Cedar Breaks

Cold. Last night a skiff
of snow. So I'm
up at five, make
a fire. Watch the sky
               unbuild.
I mean, I'm
drinking coffee
        by myself. Shivering.
And I'm cold.
    So it's time, you
    wonderful son
of a bitch. Get on up.
          I'm ready.
            Now.

Dead Horse Point

A band of wild desert ponies was herded onto the point, the best of the "broomtails" were culled for "cow service" and the rest were left to return to the range. Confused by the peculiar topography, the horses wandered in circles, and eventually died of thirst in full view of the Colorado River, half a mile away— straight down.

Ward Roylance, *Utah: A Guide to the State*

Under the white sun
the river burned. The earth
leaned toward night.
Shadows ran red and naked
like unwinged gods,
humiliated and disheveled,
sun-bleached hair wild
and electric,
limbs stretching toward
any shelter, ditchbank or arroyo.

Dusk fingers the dried streambeds
as the light disassembles,
reaches down the desert gullies
and avenues
already filled with the shed leaves
of a dying season.
Overhead, the wild stars
flash their hooves
and flowing manes,
trapped in the space
between shadow and night,
staring at the cliffedge
into a larger darkness.

Ode beneath a Hummingbird Feeder

SAMPSON. *I strike quickly, being mov'd.*
Romeo and Juliet, 1.1.6

1

Greenflash of lightning
and memory of a red scar
etched on the golden throat
of a still afternoon.

2

Whirr of tiny wings
like a small thunder
across the redwood porch.

3

Oh, arrogant little warrior,
if I had a naked weapon
I could brandish like yours
I, too, would suffer
no foolish rival suitors
sipping at my ruby fount.

Blowup Site, Williamson's Ranch

Sacred to the Memory of
Oscar Morris
Beloved son of Amasa M. and P. E. Philps
LYMAN
Born at Florence, Neb.
Dec. 16, 1847
Killed by explosion of boiler
in Red Creek Canyon Iron Co. Utah
Oct. 22, 1874

A place where shadows rest in thick grass
and a brook begins its crawl through meadow.
Each time I come here a different kind of light
separates morning and evening, crashes
the blue arc of sky and crumbles upon the earth.
A different bird calls and I am never sure
the name I hear. Windswept grass
a tangled pattern, water always rushing
down and away, the only permanence
change. Delicate blue flowers, last year
a columbine, wilting in sharp autumn light.

Today I can believe there are blossoms
up- and downstream so beautiful, so fragrant
the mind leaps to the places where they nod.
Behind me a cold breeze whimpers
from the hill. It searches the underbrush,
follows the brook. Floundering,
the north end of the meadow falls to canyon.
Water drops and flows away, courses
its irreversible journey to lowland, a quiet pond
by the still place where stone monuments
lean against the wind.

While Walking (v)

Luke 18:16

Do you think the rocks are listening to us?
I don't know. Do rocks hear?
The ones that are alive do.

Lightning above the North Fields:
Still Life with Rhyming Pronouns

Agreement at variance with itself:
adjustment under tension...

Heraclitus

Running on the graveled road
joyously. A small rain, like dew,
all afternoon and an owl

lumped in sodden plumage,
tangled in the sleep
of Russian olives. Clouds rush. Suddenly

a great flash, the reverberation.
Road clings to the shoes. Memory:
Max Cannon and his bay

gelding near Beryl Junction
a hundred yards from shelter
that year. A fieldmouse

scuttles under glistening barbed wire
into the thick redolence of sage. Smile,
or the fancy of smile,

imagining the scrim of dream
split by a phosphorescent glow,
rumble in the great vault,

cry and flutter of wet wings.
"Who, who?" *Is it you?*
"No, not I, no, not I," my thin reply.

On Finding a Drone Bee
and a Painted Lady Butterfly
in the Same Claret Cup Cactus Blossom

> *How reluctantly*
> *the bee emerges from deep*
> *within the peony.*
>
> Bashō

The red light's on,
lady's on the table

and the first john
is the Apostle Paul, confused celibate,
lost drone, missionary

from the Queen of Heaven
who thinks he's found
the Holy Grail, the flying nun

on the brink of damnation,
a fallen angel in the honky-tonk

primed for an afternoon wallow,
blown off course
and dumped in the bordello

knee deep in agua miel,
his personal challenge from God.

Cedar Mountain

For some it must be thunder. The mass
of clouds piling over the mountains,
great dark-bellied sky
crackling with ragged light. Deer
rushing through the fragile spaces
we call silence toward a groaning sanctuary
of swaying pine. High meadow
drenched with rain.

For others fragrance. Moist earth
almost forgotten over winter,
a frail scent of budding aspen.
Bubble of willow springs. Bees
hovering delicate pink and white
blossoms spreading an emerging meadow
through rotting snow.

While Walking (VI)

Job 29:5

Are all the rocks alive?
No. But some of them are.

Field Trip: Grand Canyon, North Rim

*What we observe is not nature itself, but nature
exposed to our method of questioning.*

Werner Heisenberg

"Therefore, students, the air I breathe here, then, is relative and quantum:
an abstract entity with dual aspect, which falls away into the place I call
distance, which I intuit. As the sound of the river rises, particles move in
frequencies proportional to their energies, which, scientifically, is air in the
cavity of the gorge resonating with the speed of its vibration, produced by
imposition of orderly alternations of compression and decompression,
referred to as waves, on the natural order of the distribution of the mol-
ecules of the air, which is the opposite of the natural state of disorder, or
entropy, in which the molecules usually exist, unless energy is applied to
force them into the more ordered state. This energy, then, is released, or
better, transferred, by the action of gravity, a force, on the mass of the
river's water, impacting the rocks, the water, any existing flora, and the
waves themselves. The water remains unseen, the canyon cradling it in its
distance is translated as depth, held in place by gravity. The river flows
westward through space, not separate but intimately connected with time,
which forms a four-dimensional continuum curved by mass. Beyond the
near distance the red wall of the south rim rises from the absence which is
presence invisible, innumerable photons racing before the eye at the speed
of light, its mass nothing more than a form of energy, the red wall not a
static object but a vigorously charged pattern, a process involving the energy
which manifests itself as the particle's unified body, computed by multi-
plying that mass by the speed of light squared, the space about it bent, its
curvature depending on the physical volume of the object, time as well
affected by its presence, flowing at a different rate through different matter
in different temporal sequences, the entire structure of space-time depend-
ing on the distribution of matter in the universe which is, then, finally and
ultimately, a dynamic, organic, inseparable entity which always includes
the observer in an essential way."

A man in green walking shorts, black socks, and brown wingtip shoes
stands beside me, staring into the canyon. His legs above his socks are very
white. I suspect he has come here for vacation, probably with his family
who did not wish to walk the quarter-mile distance to the point. We do

not speak. I do not look at his face. He turns, moves away, and we part like deer in an immutable forest. Beyond the south rim the far distance bends into horizon, fades into pale blue sky with its tatters of white cirrus clouds, falling away like breath.

While Walking (VII)

Proverbs 23:24

Do the stars sing?
Yes.
In which language?
They sing in every language. Even the ones we don't know.

Mountain Meadows

No. 17

Erected   *1932*

MOUNTAIN MEADOWS
A FAVORITE RECRUITING PLACE ON THE
OLD SPANISH TRAIL

IN THIS VICINITY SEPTEMBER 7TH, 1857, OCCURRED
ONE OF THE MOST LAMENTABLE TRAGEDIES IN THE
HISTORY ANNALS OF THE WEST. A COMPANY OF ABOUT
140 EMIGRANTS FROM ARKANSAS AND MISSOURI LED
BY CAPTAIN CHARLES FANCHER, ENROUTE TO
CALIFORNIA, WAS ATTACKED BY WHITE MEN AND
INDIANS. ALL BUT 17 SMALL CHILDREN WERE KILLED.
JOHN D. LEE, WHO CONFESSED PARTICIPATION AS
LEADER, WAS LEGALLY EXECUTED HERE MARCH 23RD,
1877. MOST OF THE EMIGRANTS WERE BURIED IN
THEIR OWN DEFENSE PIT. THIS MONUMENT WAS
REVERENTLY DEDICATED SEPTEMBER 10TH, 1932,
BY THE UTAH PIONEER TRAILS AND LANDMARKS
ASSOCIATION AND THE PEOPLE OF SOUTHERN UTAH.

A shadow crosses the moon.
An owl slices the coiling wind.
Dark mice scamper over the cold earth.
A yellowed leaf twirls, earthward.
Midnight, a trembling cottontail
Huddles beneath a juniper,
Cottonwoods lean with the wind, groan.
A frozen moon above the dusty sage,
Cold white bones. The owl alights,
All night heavy upon the branch, moans.

Canyonlands, Eden

O Hell! what do mine eyes with grief behold?
                Paradise Lost, 4.358

Russian thistle, goatheads,
and redroots

line the scraped streets
of the failed
Desert Paradise subdivision

clutching a derelict's treasure
of broken bottles, smashed concrete,

an abandoned '64 Ford Fairlane,
iron rebar and twisted metal roofing,
a rusted bedspring,

half sheets of pressed wood
warped and bloated

in the Utah sun,
and a child's naked doll
staring from a septic ditchline
into the pale sky.

The project's dancing brook
gagged with tamarisk,

tatters of colored grocery bags
hang limp as abandoned surrender flags
from the barbed wire
surrounding the ruined compound.

Out of a blue ceiling
ripe with sunlight

huge windborne snowflakes
from clouds stuffed
behind the La Sals
drift over the devil's garden

like Milton's doomed angels
leaping over Heaven's wall
and falling through Chaos.

Betatakin

Locust fooled the yeis. They told him he and his friends could come to Fourth World if he would sit in the same place four days. Locust left his shell and went back to Third World to tell the people what happened. On the fourth day, he crawled back into his shell and passed the test. The giants said Locust and the other beings could come and live there. In a large cave they built a ledge house with many rooms, granaries, and a kiva. There was water, tall pines, and the canyon opened to fields. Then the people grew proud and ignored the gods. They went too far. The gods became angry. The water dug into the earth and vanished. Great stones rose at night and swallowed fields of maize. In the morning the earth turned a color of dried blood and trees gnarled into bodies of twisted brush. The people began to die. A fine, red dust spread the earth and covered them. Juniper and piñon roots held it all very still. Anthropologists tell us these people were Anasazi, enemy ancestors. But they may be called Anosazi, buried ancestors. When locusts sing the night, stones open and bitter water rises in the desert. If you listen, you can hear stars call for them. The sound of their tale blossoms in the mouth.

While Walking (VIII)

Matthew 18:4

Do the stars sing in the daytime?
Yes. They always sing.
They never sleep?
That's when they sing best, when it's invisible.

Midnight Mass, Escalante

The flower moon wades
the greasy sky above Denver.

Slippery and yellow
it follows the ancient pathways
toward Canyonlands, then

Kaiparowits, the cathedral of unhewn stone,
where an evening primrose
sends its taproot
deep into whorled slickrock.

Beneath the petroglyph of a horned god
dancing across a sprawling serpent
it waits for the fat light

to open its pink blossom
and cup a single pearl of dew,

a votive candle
flickering on the altar
of Smoky Mountain.

3

This earth, the air, the heavens, the mountains, gods
and men, domestic animals and birds, vegetables and
trees, wild creatures and worms, flies and ants, are
nothing but the water under solid conditions.

Chandogya 7.10.1

The emanation which produced the creation of the
universe is like water gushing out from its source
and spreading over everything near.

Kabbalah

As soon as [Buddha] was born the thousand-eyed
(Indra) well-pleased took him gently, bright like a
golden pillar; and two pure streams of water fell
down from heaven upon his head with piles of
Mandara flowers.

Buddha-charita 1.27

Matins

Sueños o recuerdos?

Me gusta
cuando los cerdos
vuelan despacio
sobre mi cabeza

slowly
birdsong fills the room

sunlight pours
liquid and golden
over the sill

morning rushes
past dawn

day wakes and stretches
its long arms

and pigs float
slowly
back to earth

beneath
the crystal knees
of the gods

Five-Year Drought: Small September Cloudburst on Pine Valley

Look! The sky is leaking!

Charlie DeArmon, Post, Texas, 1949

From topland,
beaver ponds leak
across the sparkling meadow

like the sky
leaked starlight
down the valley.

Quail leak
from the oak thickets,
deer hesitate

then leak from the pines.
Trout hide beneath
leaking willowshadow

as the clouds mutter
and tremble, then leak
the afternoon rain shower.

South Gorge, Moab

1

Here beside the Colorado
my mind at anchor.
Clumps of salt cedar, red rock
suddenly bland, the great lethargic river
wallowing to Mexico.
                          Light so sharp
my eyes pour. A day or a week past
the man Anyman named the universe
idiosyncratic, thought solipsistic,
and worth loss. His concept
that the perceived diminishes the known
and from that one proceeds to the invented,
this mass of stone like campfire ashes
a remnant of a conceived idea, ossified.

Today by the thick, sliding water
I stare through my eyes through
a millennium of river fog through a blaze
of autumn light into the book of life
carved in red rock: the petroglyph
of a mastodon, trunk lifted,
issuing trumpet frozen in stone.

2

Four hundred miles away
a book on a shelf tells me the elephant
disappeared from this continent
20,000 years ago.
                          On a lower shelf
two feet to the left, another
says the Anasazi began their rock art
one thousand years back.

The distance numbs my brain,
words like pebbles
sink in the waters of my mind.

3

Tonight distance will dissolve.
                              And my
questions of time and perception,
blue sky, red rock, cedar and river.
Did the artist see or carve from legend?
How ancient the sigh of canyon wind?
What depth this muddy water, intolerable
except for the image of river within
and the name of the great creature
and the chiseler of stone it calls
in the night, all this perhaps nothing more
than an elegy of misconception
petrified in memory?

While Walking (ix)

> 1 John 4:4

You have to listen hard.
At night?
All the time. It's not hard. It's just not easy, either.

On the Drowned Town of Thistle
beneath the Lake Caused by the Great Mudslide

There is another world
but it is in this one.
            Paul Éluard

Something
in me wants to go there

and stand in the doorway
of a small house

where a man and woman inside
whom I know I've never seen before

tell me they remember
me as a child

and I remember them
just as I knew I would

once beneath a time
in Thistle. Inside the gush

of cold mountain water I see
blue and white columbines.

The mountain huddles above
and ducks paddle and mutter

in its reflection. There
where light is swallowed

by the pouring stream
and the village betrayed

by the transparent skin of sky
hovering above and below

I listen always
for the invisible voices

that bind the dual world
and without which

all is black
lakewater.

Roots

Some send them out like arms,
stretching for any fingerhold,
piton crevice, crack, or nook.
Limber pine work that way.
Others make their living like moles
burrowing just under the surface,
upheaving sidewalks and driveways,
drinking deeply from cisterns,
sewer pipes, waterways.
Mulberries are notorious basement
safecrackers. Cottonwoods, the great
waterhogs, suck small streams
down into the earth by day,
listen to the gurgle of the waters
as they rise in the night. Bristlecones,
the tenacious ancient ones, thrust
their lifelines into the gnarly depths
of the mountain's bones. A few—consider
the mesquite or the bur oak—
send taproots into the heart of gravity,
the deep seep where unmapped rivers
throb in the dreamripples,
the dank and secret caverns
of our darkest imaginings.

Kolob at Evening

I went to the edge of the wood
In the color of evening...
John Haines

The color of evening washed at my feet
and I dreamed years of dying suns
buried in the west end of Kolob Lake

old fishermen on their gray rocks,
beaver and swallow mating in the eclipse
of twilight and dusk
sink in the splashing reflection
to the meadow beneath the mirror
where fat trout graze like hogs
on September alfalfa

a subterranean world of sunken campfires
where I sit before black ashes
and drink lakewater from a rusted cup
while the sun falls and drives the fish
upward to explode into night
a rainbow of gods leaping to swallow the moon.

While Walking (x)

Ecclesiastes 4:13

You have to listen. All the time. Even when you're not.
I see.
That's right. You can listen that way, too.

On the Gift of an Acorn
Picked Up at the Site of Thoreau's Cabin

I have travelled a good deal in Concord
Henry David Thoreau

Harney Peak is the center of the universe
Black Elk

It's a very Thoreauvian activity
to saunter
to wander
to mess about
to hang out
to goof around with God
to find a place
to be alone   and not
to confuse that with being lonely
to live in wildness   and not
to confuse that with the need to tame
                        or civilize
                        or domesticate
                        or control
                        or dam or tunnel or plow or pave
                        or buy or sell
                                    or own   but
to walk   to think   to sing
                        until the body tires   then
to sleep
to dream of Eden
to wake here on an October dawn
                        from my *cocoon masquerading as a leaf*
                        in late middle age
                        warm and serene and golden
                        as on a bankside in autumn   reawakened
to the melodies
                        of still blue water, fragrant wind,
                        birdsong.

Tomorrow's Artifact: A Short Essay on Anthropocentric Mythopoeia

Today:
a beer can
floating in Wahweap Basin.
Coors,
Rocky Mountain Spring Water,
on course,
of course.

Rainy Day in Pine Valley

A fossilized seashell,
brain dark with it, found

at rest in the foothills outside Paragonah
near the Indian mounds,
500 miles from breaking water, 6,000 feet
above it. From this room
50 miles from the discovery,
on a shelf with clay bookends
the grand mystery, or charade:

How the gods spawned one cosmos, man
another, the sea a third, daydreamer-mythopoeticist
an additional.

How, like Antaeus,
when plucked from earth
and held to the ear
only the sound,
the texture of stone.

In a conceived apotheosis, as gods
making war on gods and then man,
the sea mindlessly disinherited earth,
these steppes, this stone shell.
Listening, consciousness stretches
through the opalescent autumn rain,
catalogs each ocean, surge and fall,
each shell in its type, place, purpose.

In the language of the sojourner,
there is a name and an allowance
for rain, shell, and ocean.
In the Logos of the desert,
where south winds fill kivas,
shape bowls in red rock
and link the seasons,

where the portraits of the gods
are carved into stone walls,
there is no name for unconceived,
unpatterned, disowned, no sufferance
for this indignity. Even here,
where dust rises on graveled roads
in days of rain, the shell *waits*.
Winds blow, the sea gathers.

Dawn Song, Last Tango in Eden

after an all-night session with Paradise Lost *and a*
sunrise reading of my daughter's translation of "Spring
Dawn" by Meng Hao-jan

Henlight and ravenclack
shattered my dreamscape
until I woke to the remains
of last night's coiled sough of wind
and rain, a thousand tangled
red and white blossoms scattered
across the floor of my garden.

While Walking (XI)

1 Corinthians 13:11

Be careful on the mountain. You could fall.
Maybe it won't let me.
The mountain doesn't care if you fall or not.
How do you know that?

Cloudburst with Duckling at the Pond's Inlet

Hey! Ustedes,
hombres y novias,
do you know
I would give
my remaining years
almost
to dance
and sing
with you
in the rain?

Rhapsody in Slickrock: A Song for the Roadrunner

homage to Abbey

Beethoven's Sixth Symphony, fourth movement
Psalms 104:32

1

Quetzalcoatl, the Morning Star, calls
the sun to come forth as did Lazarus.

Crystal and blinding,
first light pours
from the Mother of God's serape,
then gold lace, color mates with light:
red rock, blue sky, obsidian arroyoshadow—

thick golden light
brims in the sandstone basins,
its touch on the lips
sacrament
under a cloudless sky.

Now a bright alluvial fan
liquid and shimmering
like Juan Diego's roses melds
as God's arms bend and encircle
the entire goblet rim,
earth and sky fused
into the color of morning.

2

Below the horizon
great cloud formations,
ancient primordial creatures,
burrow the planet's underbelly
as they rise in darkness.
Mature, bloated, and angry,

they scuttle to the midmorning light
at the earth's rim,
clasp the bowl with gnarled fingers
and peer over the desert
like cumulonimbi gargoyles.

Small noon winds kindle
and breathe the first moist
crushed-sage scents of the desert
as the giants gather, merge and multiply.
In the distance colliding ions
swell and crack
as the thunderheads pile.
Tlaloc's army of anvil-headed warriors
throbs in ecstatic dance and
musters for the assault
upon land and sky. "Mira,"
sings a LeConte's thrasher from the yucca.
"Mira." From a mesa oak thicket
an acorn woodpecker shouts
"Mira, mira!" "Mira." "Mira!"

The gods' remuda of wild-maned mustangs
band, roil, and stampede.
Their hooves tear the desert floor
into whirlwinds and sheets
of dark sand as they
scour the mesas and arroyos,
lash the sage and rabbitbrush
into writhing flagellants,
the creosote bent penitentes prostrating
at the steps of the Guadalupe Shrine.

Thunderrumble
like distant cannonfire
shakes the desert air.
A banner sweeps
between earth and sky,
La Nublina, Walking Rain,

the beaded curtain
windswept into a soft curl.
Raindrops evaporate in the dry heat
before they reach the desert floor,
dark harbinger,
the sky half covered
with the foreshadow.
A roadrunner huddles into itself
beneath a prickly pear.

Bolts wrapped in thundershouts
assault the buttes and mesas.
Lightning volleys join earth and heaven.
A flashflood river of fire screams
through a canyon of tortured sky,
its rank ozone breath hovers
beneath the rumbling maw
of the blackened ceiling.
Earth darkens to smoky shadow,
the freighted scent of water
heavy like steam.

Midafternoon, a loud crack
like an angel's wing
snapped out of its shoulder socket.
The slipknot cord
holding the purple robe loosens.
The great cloud sags,
touches one spine of a stretching cholla,
and bursts like the belly of Judas.
With a great roar
the clouds release the rain.

3

Curtains of water,
stabs of lightning,
booming crashes of thunder,
a shrieking wind, La Llorona
wails in the darkened afternoon,

the land awash
as the cascade gushes
from the opened side of a swollen god.
Rain teems, gathers,
surges over the parched earth.

The mesas spurt waterspouts,
floodstreams course from the bluffs,
the slickrock glistens
under the mizzling sky,
lavish in the crystal rush.

Lightning explodes into a butte,
ignites the drumming rain
into vivid furor. Pitchforks
flash the sluicing downpour,
paralyze the water in midfall,

the desert glazed like porcelain,
sandstone ridges knee deep in flow,
waterfalls down their sides
gleam in this frozen moment
of an expanded time that never was.

In the next instant the squall quells,
the torrent diminishes to a shower,
a sprinkle,
then nothing at all.
The clouds move on,
                    in the distance
muttering.

4

As if a great rain-wakened serpent
slides toward the campo raso,
a huge hiss swells
from the streambed of an arroyo,
a red torrent swarms from the gully,
suddenly cast forth

from the desert's throat,
la sangre de diosito desierto
surges after a head of suds
lathered into bloody froth.

A water avalanche,
the flash flood roars
like a starving beast
fast on the spoor of a doomed prey,
its belly gorged with storm detritus,
the living and dead
carried to the Colorado,
its scream rises above the scour,
"Estupendo! Estupendo!"

The desert tsunami
cascades in a crescendo
of self-delight.

5

Blue sky in the south.
Shafts of light slice
the ragged clouds in the west
and prowl the bluff edges
like snuffing coyotes.

As if God stands in surveyance,
sombrero back, rolling a smoke,
boot up on a gray stone,
a rainbow, one foot
in the Colorado gorge runoff
and one on the shoulder
of the La Sals,
frames the steaming desert.

From a scudding cloud
a last splinter of lightning
crackles above the bootheel,
a blue diamond matchflash

on the spur rowel,
silver, glistens.
A purl of gray haze,
the air softened with the smell
of wet creosote.

6

A globe mallow river of sky floats
above the crimson desert. Nighthawks
hang on the air, then fall with a bullroar
into the spaces between light and light.
Under the red crust sprouts uncountable
writhe toward morning.

Spadefoot toads crowd the twilight
in la fiesta sapito as the males
emerge to bellow their lust
and hunger from puddles and basins.
Lovelocked females spew eggs
into the murky charca water.

Red in the bending light,
winged termites swarm the pools,
pulled from the earth
and flightbequeathed by the rain.
Cliff swallows stitch the air
and bats tumble across the shadows.

From the bluffs the shy voices
of the canyon wren float
like small waterfalls. Toads cling
to the edges of their potholes, harmonize
in counterpoint. Owlcall, dovecoo,
hawkscree, jaysquall, ravencroak

blend in an arpeggio of jubilation,
a glockenspiel of praise to the chubasco.
Coyotes from the ledges, locusts
rustle in the cottonwoods,

a murmur of distant water,
the scent of desert rain.

7

Venus nudges Mars into abeyance.
Song and incense fill the cathedral,
Red sky at night, shepherd's delight.
Under the Evening Star color and light mate:
red sky, sand, stone, shadow. No te preocupes,
paisano, all the world, todo el mundo,
ripens with rainsong tonight.

4

By air as by a thread, O Gautama! this world and all beings are strung together.

Brihad-Aranyaka 3.7.2

By the air is signified all things relating to perception and thought. And respiration corresponds to the understanding, thus to perception and thought, and also to faith, because faith is of the thought according to the perception of the understanding.

Emanuel Swedenborg

Paragonah Canyon—Autumn

Run in Darkness, Sleep in Light
W.M. Ransom

(*4:00 a.m.*)

Red bluffs open
        beneath a bloody
                eastern sky
wind pours from the toplands
scent of piñon
across oak underbrush
          sweeps away
                  in alternate currents
writhes and crashes
          against sandstone walls
          through shadows of gnarled sage
now quickly swallowed by the cracks and stains
          of high rock

          Pulled from bed
          by an old woman's cry
          her tortured laughter
          drifting from twisted canyons
          to his pillow

He rose from black sleep
to a darkened room
                    floor joists creaked
          when he stumbled toward the cookstove
          struck a tiny aspen fire

Aroma
          boiling coffee
                    woodsmoke
pulled on shoes and windbreaker
sucked the rim of his cup
stared through the window

              white sliver of dangling moon
              a handful of stars
                            splashed against
              pale morning sky

Stretched and loose
he left the house and her body
warm in sleep
to run the dusty road
to high country
                            fifteen miles
                            6,000-foot elevation thrust
                            silence
                                          morning penance

he stood in the gravel roadbed
listened
spat a benediction into dry earth
watched the horizon redden before him

                            heard the song of a meadowlark
                            rise within him
                            a quiet singing
                                          gentle in his ear

Turned and began to run

              up the road
                            slowly
                            the first hill
lumbered past houses
stiff and dark
      with sleep
across black dewslick asphalt
onto gravel
              sand
                            hardpan
Ran

                    past the place of the dead
                    silent mounds of sleep
                    where owl searches
                    the nightwind unseen
                                        unheard
followed his hard red trail
as it sprawled upward to juniper
twisting into red bluffs
where the yellow sun
struggled against sandstone cliffs

He listened
                    heard sounds
                    of his footfall
                    the only echo
                    against carved trail
Listened
                    heard breath
                    rise and fall
                    now easy

            as thick night air
            left his lungs and second wind

            crisp breeze of juniper and crimson oak
            gathered in his chest huge draughts

Listened
                    heard a steady drum
                    sound rhythm
                    the dance moved
                                    in blue lines
                    of his wrists pumping before him
                    his rising knees
                                    thighs
                                        belly
                    temples cooled now by salty droplets
                            moving within his skin

Listened

> heard a quiet singing
> one of the songs
> he has made
> lulling his mind into
>> sleep
>
> dreams

while distance
> unraveled behind
>> falling away
> like breath

(5:30 a.m.)

Ran

>> sleeping
> past the boulder that fell
> three winters back
> too large to move
>>> road rerouted

"I known them kids them kids they clumb up there they prized that thing off there with a log I bet they done that just to watch it fall I bet that's what they did"
"No Morris it just fell"
"Them kids they don't have no responsibility they clumb up there with dynamites and blowed that rock down off there I bet just so they could see what we'll do"
"No Morris it was frost it swelled up and contracted that made it break loose and down it came"
"I bet them kids is watching right now to see what we'll do just to see how we'll get around this damrock if you look up there I bet they're watching us"
"It fell Morris that's all nobody made it it did it by itself"
"I bet they got telescopes and spectaculars and they're up there right now looking at us to see what we'll do well let's see what they think of this I'll show them"

94

dropped his pants and drawers
bent over and clasped his ankles
turned on an axis full circle
the toplands staring down
at the double eclipse
full moon

blue graffiti spraypainted across its sides

Go home Prunies
California Sucks
Watch for Falling Rocks
Kill Roy was here

through the narrow hallway
of tangled oak

Heard
                                        deer
            rouse and crash underbrush
                                        mythic
            gigantic in bounding fear
            liquid grace
Heard
                        eyes lowered
                        to earth
                        saw rocks
                                sand
                                        chuckholes
                        spoke only to his feet
                        strike there
                        there
                                there
his mind singing
                        dreaming
                                        asleep
                        Saw a woman
                        her body pale   soft
                        warm in slumber

two children   Lumps
twisted in bedsheets
noses flattened against mattresses
buttocks thrust upward
like pointing fyce

Sang
        a song for them
        for himself

Felt cool shadows
where granite rose above red bluffs
blocked sun
Heard a trickle
stream dancing beside his trail
turning its pebbles
counting its wealth
                into smooth round stones
        berries here
                        and thin stalks they clip
                        and carry away for tea

                cure anything. you had thrash? it'll cure thrash.
                it'll take off sore, cure head colds, help you sleep
                at night. keep hangnails and ingrown toenails off.
                you won't get blisters you drink this. give it to
                your wife, cures all female ailments. never
                heard of anybody drink this getting cancer.
                drink it anytime you feel poorly. cure anything.
                i know. i had it all. cured me.

Above
        somewhere
the place where they say a development will come
                roads
                houses
                condominiums
                septic tanks
clustered on the red hillside
near the spring where the town below

struggles to hold a steady flow
to fill the reservoir
for each dry
       summer

Walter: Is there any other business to come before this meeting?

Barlow: Shouldn't we ought to talk about the water?

Walter: Yes.

Barlow: We're low again this year, aren't we?

Walter: Yes.

Barlow: Well, shouldn't we be trying to conserve a little here and there?

Walter: Yes.

Barlow: Well, how do you feel about the lawn watering? Shouldn't we be holding that down?

Walter: Yes.

Barlow: In fact, if we'd shut off the lawn watering we might be able to keep some of the muddy water out of the tank, wouldn't we?

Walter: Yes.

Penny: It would be nice to be able to have a drink of clear water.

Unidentified: Yes, it would.

Barlow: Can I make a motion that we don't allow lawn watering until we can get past all this?

Walter: Yes.

Carlene: You can make all the motions you want but you can't enforce anything.

Barlow: Can't we?

Carlene: No you can't. Isn't that right?

Walter: Yes.

Carlene: I grew my lawn and I'm not having it to burn up. And you can't make me stop. I'll water it all I want to. As long as I pay my water bill I can use as much as I want anytime I want. Isn't that right?

Walter: Yes.

Barlow: But...

Carlene: You can't stop me. You try. You just try. I'll sue you.
You'll see. There's nothing you can do, I'll water my lawn all I want.
I'll go water it right now if I want to.
Barlow: You mean we can't stop the watering?
Walter: Yes.

Sang
     an image of a face unseen
man who came
                    with green paper
and tongue lined with illusions

"It won't change anything. The whole subdivision will be above town, out
of sight. The only effect you'll feel or see will be the money it brings in.
Right here's where it will come. Right to your pocket. Now you tell me if
you can afford to turn that down."

A bitter song
                         dry grass and south wind
human figures
                         crawling the summertime earth
searching
                         gathering
                                        carrying away

(*6:05 a.m.*)

Oak yields to piñon
trail shifts
          east   slopes upward

He felt muscles tighten
beads drip from hair to face
onto chest
          trickle down his belly

Aside
                    tattered brown sack
                    split down one seam
                    fluttered

                    a dozen Coors cans scattered
                    before it
                    along the hillside
                    Republican beer
closed his eyes
            they passed behind

    Fabulous, said June, gorgeous. I come up here every time I can and
    just drive so I can see it. I know every rock in this road, every turn.
            Threw his beer can out the window
            Lit a cigarette
    This here's God's country. When He made this country He just
    stopped after that. Get me another of those beers, will you?
    Fabulous.

Legs lifted him to the next plateau
down and up again
The earth swells and rolls

Saw

                    before him
                            water
                                    cold springs
                    bent and lapped

Saw

                    tracks
                    by the gurgling springs
                    deer and sign of
                    a raccoon
                    pawprint in mud

Saw

                    in the moving stream
                    tiny creatures
                    scuttle
                            dart

Rose and ran

Slept

saw black words
            language of man in the crystal waters

Dear Editor:
        Frankly, I don't give a damn about the woundfin minnow, do
you? Tell me, what is a woundfin minnow? What does it look like?
What does it do? Do you know? I don't.

        But I do know what an ecologist looks like. Don't you? Long
hair, dirty fingernails, and an American flag sewn on his butt.
Remember? Now you tell me, what does this ecologist and this
woundfin minnow have in common? Does either one work? Does
either one pay taxes? What do they do?

        I'll tell you what they do: nothing. I'll tell you what they have
in common: they both stir up the

Waters muddied
pawtracks filled with thick slime
                            still
creatures writhed
                twisted
floated belly-up in ooze
                    Dreamed

                sharp lines
                straight lines
                giant concrete dams
                oil derricks
                strip mines
                                a monotonous geometry
                spreading across
                the earth
                from still waters
                    lines rose
                    surged from the mud
                    where creatures sprawl
                        still

Dreamed

                  crisp air
                  pink and yellow air of morning
                  clutching high peaks
                        dark air
                        thick dark air
                        crawling the bottomlands
                        holding the earth heavy and still
                        in shuddering slumber

feeding the lines
                black lines

Dreamed

                  iron fingers
                  raking the earth's belly
                                under
                  a jellied sky
                        searching
                  regions where frost tides
                                raise
                  great stones in the silent mounds of buried gods
                        sleeping
                  a shattered jawbone carried away
                  smoldering
                        above a hoarfrost-glazed
                                    wasteland

black shadows weaving
Spider Woman's insane laughter
into a gray blanket of twilight

Saw

                  men flap their wings
                  flail the still air
                  the walled room

"It's power this is about. And money that power can bring."

He
                    opened his eyes

Saw

                    a white bone
                    shinbone of a deer
                                        cracked
                    broken beside his rising trail
                    the dark hollow looked
                    into his eyes

Ran on

                    upward

"We can't be letting these foreigners or them environmentalists in
Washington tell us what to do with our land. Our water. We own it, we
can do whatever we want to do with it. That's our business, not theirs.
That's our decision. And we don't need their help making it. We don't
need them bringing in their ideas on how we're supposed to live. We don't
need them bringing in nothing."

                    Above   a scree

Saw

                    a feather on the red earth
                    fluttered loose
                                        spiraled down
            Day of the Loon
                            Morning of the Owl

(*6:45 a.m.*)

Opened his eyes
            Looked before him
        Smiled
            Panted
                bent forward

climbed the last hill
                    before the reservoir
                    Rhythm of his footfall
                                        faster
                    now faster

Stopped
                    Stood on the hill
                       above the dam
                    above the flat blue
                    rippling pond

Heard
                    sounds of his breath rising
                                        falling

Saw
                    a silver flash
                    broken image
                    spreading circle
                    on the water

            man in the boat
                            waved

        why you do that? he said at Linda's store one day
        why you run up that mountain
        ain't you too old to be doing that? Major Chase said
        but I didn't say anything
        Billy said running up that mountain I imagine
        you're like a fish trying to swim upstream in floodwater
        he laughed but I didn't say anything
        he's running he said but he's not getting anywhere
        Major Chase said no he gets up there I've seen it
        with my own eyes and Billy said oh yeah?

waved back
            lifted a stringer
            of glistening fish
            in the morning sun

See him? the man in the boat said to his dog.
Up there. On the trail. There he is again.
Waved.
You ever run in a race? I'll bet you
Could beat anybody.
                    Never had the guts
to say, No. I'm slow. I never won anything
in my life.   Waved again.
That's not why I do it.

Looked west

         down the canyon
         across piñon

Saw

         Buckhorn Flat rise
         to gray mountains
         fall to the great basin
         rise and fall and rise
                 again
         to mountains far away
               blue

Dear Sir,

     I enjoyed your lecture and reading at the college last night but I
have a comment I want to make. Whatever happened to poetry? In my
opinion what you read was prose, not poetry. What happened to rhyme?
What happened to meter? My favorite poet is Frederick Service. What
happened to Frederick Service?

Mistah Service he dead

     Frederick Burns
      Frederick Frost
    Robert Nietzsche
  "a penny for the old guy"

    No
      for 2 cents I'd
      forget it
      2 cents not worth nothing
      no more

      nothing's worth nothing no more
      with that circus in the White House

      big top too far away
      all we need's an elephant and calliope

      we got the clowns and gorillas and peanuts
      and the shell game and oil crews and stripminers

      and the future bodes ill

   In conclusion, in my opinion Marlowe was an homosexual. The
way he set with his legs crossed and his palms up with a yellow complex-
tion. And he was wanting Kuntz, a man with a blad head, like the skulls
on his fence, who was a fallic symbol. It was a good book. But I don't like
reading about the homosexuals. It isn't necessary. But I enjoyed it, what I
understood.

Looked south
     where the trail lifted
     above the shining blue water
Saw
     deep green and blue
     pine and spruce
Heard
     his breath
     gentle

Heard

      old woman's song
      whisper
      from trembling aspen

Turned and began to run

Dreamed

      meadowlark
      song from the basin below
      from the wooden fence he made
      outside the room where he slept

Dreamed

      an image of song

Pulled his eyes from two feet
shattering dry
         red earth
to basin below

Saw

      men who sat in a room with walls
        many men carrying voices
        in their sleeves
              pockets
      Sounds of ice and fire
        earth splitting
              erupting
        unbuilding into
              endless sleep
      Men who raised their arms
        opened their hands
        offered empty night

We thought it was wonderful. Thought
it was our patriotic duty to support the tests,
to watch. Went out past the stockyards
out on a west hill and watched: pretty,
orange and red like the sun
              rising in the west

Afternoon the bomb clouds drifted over
      once you've seen one you'll never forget it
We were hicks in New York City
craning our necks to see the skyscrapers
      watching the clouds

                floating like dreams

      Annie
      Baneberry
      Climax
      Diablo
      (Dirty) Harry
      Dog
      Hood
      Met
      Mighty Oak
      Moth
      Nancy
      Plumbbob
      Priscilla
      Simon
      Smoky
      Turk
          et cetera
          et al.

126 detonations
      27 January 1951–11 July 1962

      Downwinders

A blue-coated man
beat the air to clear his voice
a pathway
                Spoke
      his lips tight   almost unmoving
      eyes thick   almost glazed
"This next battle, we feel, will be for the right to inherit the earth."

By that night we could already feel it
      headaches, stomachs upset
where my wife's skin showed
      where she wasn't covered up
                           bright red

She went in to shampoo
there was a loud scream
I ran
      :all of her hair laying in the sink

"I wish we had more informed, patriotic people here tonight who had taken the time to read a book written by Marx and Lenin titled *The Communist Manifesto* that predicts a great battle fought for the conquest of the world by the Soviet Union."
      "Senator," he said,
      "I believe that book was a treatise
      on economics
      and I believe it was written
      by Marx and Engels
      and I believe it was published
      in 1848
      before either Mr. Lenin or the Soviet Union
      were born
      and I believe I know this because I actually
      read the book."

Sir,
defunct

                sir who used to
                fly those ohsohuge silver

                                airplanes
and (they said) had the sense to get out of office while the getting out
   was good

                                General
you sure loved giving those speeches, we could all of us surely see that for
   a fact
                    but what I want to know is
              did you only puke all over the inside
of the space shuttle
Mister Senator

            The basin
            desert floor
            etched with black lines
            smooth parallel geometry
            a racetrack
            vexing nightmare
            to dreamless sleep

"I have a new baby," she said, "and I wonder what kind of a future he will
have. I wonder how this can ever be beaten back into a plowshare." It was
her first time on television and she was frightened. But she spoke.

        Sick. After a year we took her to Salt Lake.
        It was a tumor in her brain
                        size of a small grapefruit
        "Now I've heard talk tonight about the
        land mode, the air mode, and the sea
        mode. What I want to know is
        why doesn't somebody talk about the co-mode."
                A prophet.
                Just a day gone I said, no
                I don't believe that.
                I believe the age of prophecy
                is closed, gone, over.

Took her two years to die
The hardest part
:waking up that little girl
to tell her Mother was gone

The clouds deliberately set loose to drift predetermined over
    "A low use segment of the population"
            Declassified Atomic Energy Commission Memo,
            United States of America

a trout swimming upstream in floodwater

        "I will not give imprimatur to that."
                Your what? How you spell that thing?
                What he say?
                I think he said no I think

"Ask not what? What I can what what? Bull, I say. I don't want nothing
from the goverment. And I don't want to give nothing else to the gover-
ment. I gave him my brother in Germany, a boy in Korea, and a grandson
in Vietnam. A wife to the bomb tests. And a third of ever dollar I make.
That's enough. I want the goverment the hell out of my life and the mail
delivered on time. That's all. Don't ask nothing else. I done give at the
office. Every month. Every week. Every day. Don't ask no more. There's
nothing else left."

        Cyclops hath not stereopsis

Meadowlark cackled
            the old woman's voice
                            sound
        of alfalfa
        rotting in the sun
        corn dying
        on its stalk
        higher and higher
        frozen in moonlight
                        silence

Looked away
Looked

                              upward to aspen
                              bleeding across the topland
                              High country

Ran

Felt

                                   sunlight and shadow
                         Mountain breeze cooled his face
                         Wet hair exploded into day
                         A maze of shimmering shadows
                         crosshatched red earth
His feet plodded
                    heavy
on the helpless earth
left no footprints

He
    lumbered
gasped
        fought his way
to high country
                Aspen

(*7:30 a.m.*)

Looked

                    to the side
Saw

                    hunting camps
                    deserted frames
                    of steel chairs
                    tossed away
                                rusting

         piles of charred cans in ash
         scraps of bleached paper and cloth
         searching the underbrush

Black lines
crawled their way up cool white aspen bark

Dear editor

I see where the legislature is passing a bill making it a
CRIME to "deface, mark, or write upon any object, personal or
private on any public land or in any forest."

To the legislature. Sir. Have you ever been to Capital Reef?
And witnessed the names and dates the pilgrims carved when they
passed? Over a hundred years ago. That sir is history. And right
down the bend are the pictures the indians drew which was their
way of signing they're names. No one knows what it means. That
is history.

One day my great grandson will walk through those rock
halls. Imagine his wonder if he looks up and sees the name of his
great great grandfather, his surprize. And his proudness. Or if he
finds the name of his great great grandfather carved in history on
the bark of an aspen tree. Can you fell the lump in his throat?
That sir is history. And I fell I have a right to be part of it.

I fell it is my GOD GIVEN RIGHT as a TAXPAYING
AMERICAN to be a part of history. And the legislature has no
right to deny that. That is communist. So I urge you to vote
against it. We must protect our taxpaying rights.

Looked
                    to the side

Saw

                    logging roads
                    etch the forest floor
                    slash bulldozed into charred heaps
                    ragged pyres
                                        an abandoned tire blitzed
                    thrashed
                            forgotten
                    a young pine bent earthward
                    its needles yellowed
                    falling to decay

the poem found on a piece of paper
in an abandoned hunting camp near Blowup:
      Alas. Poor Utah.
      Weep for Utah.
      So far from heaven.
      So terribly close to California.

          Now Texas.
            And
                  they will Not be
                  misunderestimated
                      nosir

Looked
              to the side
Saw
              in the sparkling stream
              tiny creek
        a cigarette pack red and white and drowning
        two beer cans dead submerged gathering moss

Looked away
Looked upward
Heard
              a winddrift from the topland
              Spider Woman's weeping
              red cliffs dry
                    silent
              Ran on

Slept
Dreamed

| Saw clusters | crystals | fold inward |
| draw him | pull him | inside |

Saw

| trees | red earth | blue sky |
| shatter | crumble | fall |

                    rush inside
                                saw his song dissolve
                                            flow inside

Dreamed

Saw

                    men cross the earth
                    the red earth
                    in wagons
                                on horseback
                    Men and Women
                                Children

                    Him? Oh, he's our ninth.
                    Heber Zinas Prince his name.
                    Yes, it's the Lord's will, His plan.
                    No, these are hand-me-downs.
                    Who can afford new things these days?
                    The Lord will provide.
                    He has a plan and we follow His ways.
                    The Lord always knows what's best.

"Kinda screwed up in India, I expect," said Henry Webb
(and I'd just said the age of prophecy/prophets was dead)

                    their faces lowered
                    eyes closed
                    Crossed the earth
                    frozen streams
                                desert
                    pushed their wagons
                    their oxen
                    over the earth
                    down its canyons
                    up its granite slopes

Dear Editor:

My family and I passed through your State this year, vacationing. We went out of our way to see your "famous" Color Country: Bryce Canyon, Cedar Breaks, Zion Canyon, the Grand Canyon. We were appalled by the commercial exploitation of what is nothing more (or less) than sheer, preventable soil erosion.

To call a condition of this kind beauty is a travesty. To make a Monument or National Park out of this is gross and crass capitalistic opportunism of the lowest nature and

> left their dead
> in silent mounds
>   sleeping
> They came

Heard

> cries
>   moans
> cut the night air
> They came

Saw

> their houses
>   cities
> rise from the red earth
> sprawling silent land
> temples
> reaching for distant sky

"We pray before all public meetings."
"Why?"
"Because this is one nation under God-Indivisible."
"Why not silent meditation?"
"Because it is tradition in this society."
"He's Jewish."
"He is a minority."
"He's Hindu."
"He is a minority."
"He's something else. Buddhist, Christian, Deist."

"He is a minority. The will of the majority is dominant. Now bow your head."

And you pray.

Dear Heavenly Father I pledge allegiance

Just as I am
without one plea
but that

oh

I believe
oh

High country

Gaia

I come

"The Lord our Father." "Who said?" "What?" "He." "He?" "That it's a he." "Who?" "God." "Gawd?" "Yes." "Our Father in Heaven? Heavenly Father?" "Yes. YHVH Elohim. Lord of gods. Plural in Genesis 1. Gods, little g." "Hallowed be His name." "Which name?" "The Lohrd Gawd!" "And in Judges? Where it says Spirit of the Lord?" "The Holy Ghost." "Later. They hadn't invented it yet. Spirit of the Lord there. Did you know that's a feminine noun in Hebrew?" "What is your name? Tell me your name. You tell me your NAME!"

I come

Saw

their progeny
the many-wived men's progeny
spread the earth
scratching   scraping   unbuilding
and building

They came

Saw

their strife

wars

blood seeping into the red earth

This is a closed society you must understand. A conservative society. Perhaps aggressively conservative, perhaps aggressively backward. The attitude is, don't try to change us, we'll change you. As an outsider you have no opinion worth hearing or tolerating. It's like a great invisible wall has been built around their own Cathay and it is watched over by the great glass eye of their God, and they'll by their heaven keep their sheep inside and they'll by the threat of your heaven keep the wolves locked out. The last time that happened the people inside finished the wall, went to sleep and woke up five hundred years later. And the rest of the world walked right on by. That can be frightening if you're one of those who has been walled inside.

Saw

> wagons
> circled wagons
asleep in the high mountain meadows

heard
> shouts of a bloody dawn
voices of patriarchs
rise above the green and yellow grass

heard
> cries
> > pain
death sob of one hundred twenty pilgrims
fade into silence
> > sleep
saw
> the Indian farmer brought again
> > to the meadow
> > silent parched earth

"Yawguts them Indins called him. Means bawlbaby. They said he cried the whole time for that Fancher bunch. I don't believe it. I don't know how come them Indins call him that. They liars, I expect. They don't believe in God."

heard
　　　words
his pleas for his children

　　　"Now this, students, is the General Reference Room. You should all become acquainted with this room. Here you can find newspapers and magazines. We keep our maps here. And this is a dictionary. This is where we keep all the words."

heard
　　　words in the wind
　　　　　　　　　　perjury
of his adopted father
condemn the sealed son to silence
　　　　　　　　　　stone

"Words. That's all I hear in here. Is words. Just words. They don't mean nothing. It don't mean nothing at all."

heard
　　　shots as he sat atop his own coffin

"You mean that thing ain't a man?"
"He's becoming one."
"Like that?"
"Exactly."
"All them muscles."
"That he must give up to become."
"And he goes up on top?"
"Above the Gates of Hell."
"How come up there?"
"That's where the statues of the naked women are."

toppled back inside
echoes against the topland
　　　　　　　across horizons
across time
saw
　　　　　his seed scattered
　　　　　　　　　nameless

They tore his house in Washington, Utah, down. It was haunted they feared. Used the stones to build a dam on the Virgin River for a reservoir. Buried him in Panguitch so people would leave his grave alone. That was his last wish, sort of. He said, "Center on my heart, boys. Don't mangle my body." So they did.

        over the dry earth

He

                  stretched forth his hand
                    pushed away the dream
                    the crystals
                    Pushed away
                    the old woman's howl
                    her cry
                    Pushed away the silence
                    falling sky
                    Pushed away the red dreams
                    of his inheritance

(8:00 a.m.)

Stood
    silent on the mountain
Looked
      down on Horse Valley
                golden
        glittering in ripe autumn
Felt
    his blood rise and flow
    within his veins
            Felt
    his breath warm and clean
    under a pale deep sky
            Felt
    his legs firm
        solid against red earth
Felt
    his mind empty the miles
    loose scraps of song and dream

illusions
 and memory
float beneath him
 drifting
spiraling into the golden aspen

 Threw back his shaggy head
 stared into endless sky

While Walking (XII)

Isaiah 11:6

Are you ready to go home?
I thought that's where we are.

Behold, the heaven and the heaven of heavens is the
Lord's thy God, and the earth also, with all therein is

Deuteronomy 10:14

The earth is the Lord's, and the fulness thereof, the
world, and they that dwell therein

Psalms 24:1

For the earth is the Lord's, and the fulness thereof

1 Corinthians 10:26

So quietly the world

Eleanor Wilner

And what were thou, and earth, and stars, and sea,
If to the human mind's imaginings
Silence and solitude were vacancy?

Shelley, "Mont Blanc"

Requiem

More than a high-desert sun dog shimmering
above thin lines of the Canyonland's open throat
or the sift of October-flushed aspen
on a gnarled Pine Valley, Utah, morning.
More than the pink fleece of a lost primrose
bathed in twilight by a graveled roadside
or the shadow of a cornstalk petroglyph
leaning into its basalt winter.
Beyond words sliding from hollows of memory
that hold image and time in stone cups
is the yearning, the bending to morning,
the huddled ache that can never be soothed
by moonlight or spring rains or crimson oak,
only by tomorrow's sunrise.

ABOUT THE AUTHOR

Over the course of a fifteen-book career, David Lee has written a poetry unlike any in American letters. His poems are informed by a background that is also unique to the world of poetry: he was a seminarian studying theology; he played semiprofessional baseball as the only white player to ever play for the Negro League Post Texas Blue Stars and was a knuckleball pitcher for the South Plains Texas League Hubbers; he was a boxer; he has raised hogs and worked as a laborer in a cotton mill; and he earned a Ph.D. with a specialty in the poetry of John Milton. After thirty-two years of teaching at Southern Utah University he recently retired as the chairman of the Department of Humanitites, Languages, and Literature.

Lee was named Utah's first Poet Laureate, and has been honored with grants from the National Endowment for the Arts and the National Endowment for the Humanities. His awards include the Mountains & Plains Booksellers Award, the Western States Book Award, and the Utah Governor's Award for lifetime achievement in the arts.

The Chinese character for poetry is made up of two parts: "word" and "temple." It also serves as pressmark for Copper Canyon Press.

Founded in 1972, Copper Canyon Press remains dedicated to publishing poetry exclusively, from Nobel laureates to new and emerging authors. The Press thrives with the generous patronage of readers, writers, booksellers, librarians, teachers, students, and funders—everyone who shares the conviction that poetry invigorates the language and sharpens our appreciation of the world.

The Allen Foundation for The Arts
Lannan Foundation
National Endowment for the Arts
Washington State Arts Commission

THE ALLEN FOUNDATION *for* THE ARTS

For information and catalogs:
COPPER CANYON PRESS
Post Office Box 271
Port Townsend, Washington 98368
360/385-4925
www.coppercanyonpress.org

NATIONAL
ENDOWMENT
FOR THE ARTS

This book was designed and typeset by Phil Kovacevich.
The typefaces used are Adobe Garamond and Scala.